3/97

18.65

A Tribute to
THE YOUNG AT HEART

H. A. REY

By Julie Berg

Published by Abdo & Daughters, 4940 Viking Drive, Suite 622, Edina, Minnesota 55435.

Library bound edition distributed by Rockbottom Books, Pentagon Tower, P.O. Box 36036, Minneapolis, Minnesota 55435.

Printed in the United States.

Cover Photo credit: Bettmann
Interior Photo credits: Bettmann

Edited by Rosemary Wallner

Library of Congress Cataloging-in-Publication Data

Berg, Julie.
    H.A. Rey / Julie Berg.
        p.   cm. -- (A Tribute to the Young at Heart)
    ISBN 1-56239-357-X -- ISBN 1-56239-368-5 (paperback)
    1. Rey, H.A. (Hans Augusto), 1898-1977 --Biography--Juvenile
literature. 2. Authors, American--20th century--biography
--juvenile literature. 3. Illustrators--United States--biogra-
phy--juvenile literature. 4. Childrens literature --authorship--
juvenile literature. 5. Illustration of books--juvenile literature.
[1. Rey, H.A. (Hans Augusto), 1898- . 2. Authors, American.
3. Illustrators.] I. Title.   II. Series.
PS3535.E924Z59   1994
813'.52--dc20   94-32229
                                            CIP
                                            AC

TABLE OF CONTENTS

Monkeyshines

Hans Augusto (H. A.) Rey was the creator of the widely popular Curious George stories. Ever since the man in the big yellow hat found George in the jungle and brought him to civilization, the little monkey has been getting into mischief. Even today, the Curious George books remain popular with children of all ages.

"George's curiosity gets him into trouble," said Margret Rey, who created the children's book character in 1937 with her husband. "But he always gets himself out of it through his own ingenuity. I suppose there's a moral in that."

In addition to writing and illustrating seven Curious George books, Rey lent his talents to many other books. He used his interest in astronomy to create two books on stargazing.

He also illustrated stories by other authors, and created puzzle and pop-up books. His books have been translated into nine languages. They have a combined sales of more than twenty million copies.

H.A. Rey, author and creator of Curious George.

Germany and Brazil

Rey was born in Hamburg, Germany, on
September 16, 1898. His parents were
Alexander and Martha Reyersbach. By the age
of two, young Rey displayed a talent for
drawing. He developed his artistic skill during
his school years, often drawing in his
sketchbook during other lessons.

When World War I broke out, eighteen-year-old
Rey was drafted into the army. He served with
the infantry and medical corps in France and
Russia from 1916 to 1919. "I did better with my
pencil than with my rifle," he stated.

When he left the army, Rey wanted to attend an
art school, but he could not afford the tuition.
Instead he attended the University of Munich

(1919-20) and the University of Hamburg (1920-23). To earn money, he created free-lance artwork in his spare time.

H.A. Rey was born in Hamburg, Germany, in 1898.

Before Rey formally finished school, family members offered him a job at their import/export firm in Rio de Janeiro, Brazil. Rey accepted. While in Brazil, he met Margret Waldstein, a young woman who had also grown up in Hamburg. The two shared an interest in art and a distaste for the Nazi government of Germany. They were married in 1935.

Fleeing the Nazis

The Reys moved to Paris where Rey began to write and draw children's books. "We had very little money," recalled Margret. For a French magazine, Rey created some cartoons in which a giraffe's neck served as a ladder and a sailboard mast.

"An editor at Gallimard [a French publishing house] called us and asked if we could do a children's book," Margret said. "We did the book, and it agreed with us. Then we wrote another book, just about a monkey. We never thought it would be a series. In fact, we never wanted to do another, because series always go downhill, capitalizing on the first book." That book would eventually become the first of the Curious George series.

Rey completed several more books, often collaborating on them with Margret. Most of the books involved animals as the main characters. The Reys had no children. Their books were not designed for young readers' tastes. "We just did what pleased us," Margret said.

In 1940 the Reys were forced to flee Paris on bicycles when Nazi Germany invaded France.

They took with them only a small amount of food and some of Rey's manuscripts. Escaping France, they traveled to America. In 1940, H. A. Rey became a naturalized U.S. citizen.

Monkeys, Monkeys Everywhere

When he was growing up, Rey lived near the Hagenbeck Zoo in Hamburg. Visiting the zoo often, he developed a fondness for a variety of exotic animals. "I was more familiar with elephants and kangaroos than with cows or sheep," he stated.

The first book that Rey wrote and illustrated, *Cecily G. and the Nine Monkeys*, displayed his love of animals. In the story, Cecily G. is a lonely giraffe (the "G" in her name stands for giraffe) who has been separated from her family. The nine monkeys are a family that has been driven out of their home by woodcutters. The monkeys are searching for a new place to live. One of the monkeys is named George.

Elephants at the Hagenbeck Zoo in Hamburg, Germany, where Rey grew up.

Cecily and the monkeys meet and instantly become friends. Cecily invites the monkeys to stay in her home, sleep in her long giraffe's bed, and play inventive games with her. In addition to using her long body as a bridge, the monkeys ski down her neck, use her as a seesaw, parachute off her head with their umbrellas, and even use her as a makeshift harp during a concert.

Cecily G. and the Nine Monkeys is the American version of *Raffy and the Nine Monkeys*, which Rey also wrote. *Raffy* was published in England. In *Raffy*, Rey used the name Zozo instead of George. When the editor at Gallimard saw an ad Rey had done featuring the giraffe, he asked Rey to create another children's book.

"We never expected to do children's books," Margret recalled years later. "I don't believe in the glorification of children. We loved monkeys, and the first thing we did when we went to a new city was to visit the zoo. Hans was the artist, a genius and a dreamer who loved animals. I was the midwife. I'd write the text and supervise the drawings."

Tit for Tat

The book of verse, *Tit for Tat*, came out in 1942. In the story, a boy named Matt unthinkingly abandons a turtle lying on its back. Professor Appleby uses a device called turn-a-vision, which resembles a television set, to demonstrate a reversal of human and animal positions.

Once the device is turned on, dogs are shown walking people. Also, people are shown caught in mousetraps, worn around necks as fur, and caught on hooks like fish. The book concludes:

Of course, most of us animals
Are patient and will thus
Not really think of paying back
What people do to us.

Children who view the turn-a-vision show see how the animals feel. Rey and his wife hoped their readers would be kind to animals.

Curious George

Cecily G. and the Nine Monkeys introduced readers to an important character. In listing each monkey, Rey used two words to describe the monkey named George: clever and curious. Rey found George so entertaining that he devoted an entire book to the little monkey's adventures. He titled it simply *Curious George.*

Curious George begins with George playing in his African jungle home. Rey introduces his character with this description: "He was a good little monkey and always very curious."

While playing, George notices a man, dressed in yellow and wearing a large yellow hat, watching him. Naturally, George is very curious about this man. When the man places his hat on the ground, George cannot resist the urge to investigate. Before George knows what has happened, the man with the yellow hat—the only name he is given in the books—has snatched the little monkey up and taken him back to his ship.

The man explains to George that he is taking him to the city to live in a zoo. He tells George that he may look around the boat, but to be careful and stay out of trouble. George does just the opposite and ends up falling into the ocean while trying to fly like a seagull.

Once in the city, George finds himself in more trouble. He plays with a phone and accidentally dials the fire department. The firefighters arrive, find there is no fire, and put George in jail for playing pranks. He escapes from the jail, grabs a bunch of balloons, and sails off over the city.

In the end, the man with the yellow hat finds George and takes him to his happy new home in the zoo.

The universal appeal of *Curious George* is illustrated by an incident that occurred shortly after Rey finished the book. Just prior to fleeing France, the Reys were arrested by the French police. The police suspected them of spying.

During the Reys' interrogation, an officer found the *Curious George* manuscript. He attempted to find evidence in the book that would confirm the Reys as spies. Instead, the man found himself amused and enchanted by the story of the little monkey. Thinking that the person who wrote such an innocent and funny book could not possibly be a spy, the officer released the Reys. They were able to escape the Nazi invasion.

More Monkey Business

In six more books, Rey continued George's adventures, often collaborating on them with Margret. "The share of my wife's work varies," Rey once said. "Basically, I illustrate and Margret writes."

In the series, George gets a job, rides a bike, and flies a kite—managing to cause something of a ruckus in each case. Along the way he also receives a medal, flies in outer space, and appears in a motion picture.

Rey makes it clear that George's intentions are good, but his curiosity just seems to get the best of him. Regardless of the amount of trouble George manages to get into, the man with the yellow hat always arrives in time to rescue George from disaster.

Rey also worked on two Curious George stories—*Curious George Learns the Alphabet* and *Curious George Goes to the Hospital*—that differed from his previous books. Both books attempted to be educational and entertaining.

In *Curious George Learns the Alphabet*, the man with the yellow hat teaches George his ABCs.

In *Curious George Goes to the Hospital*, George suffers from mysterious stomach pains and stays at the hospital. The staff takes him to the children's ward where he meets young boys and girls who also need medical attention.

George does not feel well at first, but after the doctors help him, he recovers and is again his old, curious self. He decides to explore the hospital and, as usual, causes a commotion.

While creating the story, the Rey's worked with the Children's Hospital Medical Center in Boston, Massachusetts. The Rey's wanted to familiarize children with hospitals, their procedures, and the people who work there. By presenting the hospital in a story with a comforting and familiar character like George, the Reys hoped to ease some of the anxiety a child entering a hospital might have.

Universal Appeal

George fascinates readers of all ages. Children love George because his appearance and behavior are similar to their lives. He has wild adventures and is sometimes punished for his antics. While his escapades always cause trouble, they usually result in some good and George is rewarded or praised.

There are many reasons why Curious George still remains popular. The most important is the ease with which young readers can identify with him. He is an animal doing the things that they would like to do.

Adults also like George. Their children can identify with him, yet because he is a monkey, they can distinguish between George's world and reality.

George is drawn in a cartoon style, one that illustrates his good nature and innocence. You see a likable monkey, with a sweet, simple face. He can look happy or sad, or maybe surprised, but he never loses the sweetness in his expression.

Plants, Pretzels, and Other Books

In addition to the Curious George series, Rey worked on several other books. He wrote and illustrated *Elizabite: The Adventures of a Carnivorous Plant*, the story of a plant with a large appetite for just about anything it can get its leaves on.

Elizabite gleefully eats insects in the wild and Scottie dogs' tails in captivity. Banished from the laboratory for her nibblings, she gulps down a burglar and is rewarded by a good life in the zoo. There, she and her four offspring are the star attractions.

Pretzel tells the story of a dachshund who is extraordinarily long. Pretzel is unhappy because his appearance does not please Greta, the female dog that he loves. When Greta gets into trouble, Pretzel's length enables him to rescue her, and she sees his true, unique beauty.

During 1951, the Reys provided a cartoon page for children in *Good Housekeeping* magazine. It featured Curious George using his British name, Zozo. Several of the incidents were later used in Curious George books.

Rey wrote and illustrated five puzzle books: *How Do You Get There?* (1941), *Anybody at Home?* (1942), *Where's My Baby?* (1943), *Feed the Animals* (1944), and *See the Circus* (1956). These books have half-page foldouts that provide the answers to questions about animal homes (such as who lives in a nest, shell, or zoo), baby animals, animals' diets, and circus animals.

Rey also combined his interests in stargazing and drawing in two books about astronomy: *Find the Constellations*, which he wrote for children, and *The Stars: A New Way to See Them*, written for adults.

For the books, which are still a resource for the amateur astronomer, Rey used material from a New Year's Eve card that showed the big dipper. It was designed by him for the year 1949. Each book features Rey's bright, colorful illustrations and a unique system—invented by Rey himself—that easily identifies the constellations.

Rey also compiled and illustrated the songbooks *Humpty Dumpty* and *Other Mother*

Goose Songs (1943) and *We Three Kings and Other Christmas Carols* (1944). In the first, Rey drew musical notes to complement the songs. For example, "Mary Had a Little Lamb" has notes that are sheep. The "Humpty Dumpty" song has eggs for notes. And "Little Miss Muffet" is accompanied by spider notes.

"Making picture books for children is the most wonderful profession I can think of," Rey once said. "Not only do you have fun doing it but your fellow men even pay you for it."

The 50th Anniversary Party

On August 16, 1977, H.A. Rey died. After his death, Margret insisted that it was impossible to continue the work alone. "Each book took a long time," she said. "All my life I spent standing behind him at his desk. I made all the movements George makes. When we had one book finished, I'd vow, 'Never again.' "

Instead, Margret spent her time overseeing quality control of Curious George merchandise. That included hats, shirts, puzzles, and dolls.

Curious George celebrated his fiftieth birthday at Harvard's Erikson Center, where Margret Rey was a research associate in childhood studies. Over the years, seven Curious George books have been translated into 15 languages, with 20 million copies in print worldwide.

The humor in H. A. Rey's books borrow the slapstick comedy of Charlie Chaplin.

A Beloved Children's Author

Rey's career as an author and illustrator spanned more than thirty years. In that time he created some of the most beloved books in children's literature.

The humor in his books, borrowed from the slapstick comedy of silent screen star Charlie Chaplin and the simple logic of comic strips, make them all the more appealing to children. Rey brought a basic sensibility to all of his books. "I believe I know what children like," Rey once said. "I know what I liked as a child, and I don't do any book that I, as a child, wouldn't have liked."

H.A. Rey, the beloved childrens author/illustrator and creator of Curious George.

Books by H. A. Rey

Zebrology, 1937

How the Flying Fishes Came into Being, 1938

Aerodome for Scissors and Paint, 1939

Raffy and the Nine Monkeys, 1939

Curious George, 1941

How Do You Get There? 1941

Au Clair de la lune and Other French Nursery
    Songs, 1941

Anybody at Home? 1942

Tit for Tat, 1942

Christmas Manger, 1942

Uncle Gus's Circus, 1942

Uncle Gus's Farm, 1942

Cecily G. and the Nine Monkeys, 1942

Elizabite: The Adventures of a Carnivorous
    Plant, 1942

Where's My Baby? 1943

Tommy Helps Too, 1943

Humpty Dumpty and Other Mother Goose
     Songs, 1943

We Three Kings and Other Christmas Carols,
     1944

Feed the Animals, 1944

Look for the Letters: A Hide-and-Seek Alphabet,
     1945

Curious George Takes a Job, 1947

Mary Had a Little Lamb, 1951

Curious George Rides a Bike, 1952

The Stars: A New Way to See Them, 1952

Find the Constellations, 1954

See the Circus, 1956

Curious George Gets a Medal, 1962

Curious George Learns the Alphabet, 1963